Carving In Soap

North American Animals

Howard K. Suzuki

4880 Lower Valley Road, Atglen, PA 19310 USA

Acknowledgments

I want to thank Ms. Lila Gilmer for carving the cougar for my book. We spent a long weekend working very hard to carve and photograph the project while she was a guest at our cabin in North Carolina. I want to give special thanks to my wife, Tetsuko, for her support on the writing of this book and for her excellent editing of the manuscript. I also want to thank her for the use of her laptop computer, without which I would not have been able to complete the book while spending the spring and summer at our cabin. I also want to thank my editor, Mr. Douglas Congdon Martin, for his help and support through the intricacies of writing and editing in today's highly computerized age.

Designed by John P. Cheek
Type set in Windsor BT/Korinna BT

ISBN: 0-7643-1292-8
Printed in China

Published by Schiffer Publishing Ltd.
4880 Lower Valley Road
Atglen, PA 19310
Phone: (610) 593-1777; Fax: (610) 593-2002
E-mail: Schifferbk@aol.com
Please visit our web site catalog at
www.schifferbooks.com or write for a free catalog.

We are always looking for authors to write books on new and related subjects. If you have an idea for a book, please contact us at the above address.

This book may be purchased from the publisher.
Please include $3.95 for shipping.

In Europe, Schiffer books are distributed by
Bushwood Books
6 Marksbury Ave.
Kew Gardens
Surrey TW9 4JF England
Phone: 44 (0)20-8392-8585; Fax: 44 (0)20-8392-9876
E-mail: Bushwd@aol.com
Free postage in the UK. Europe: Air mail at cost.
Please try your bookstore first.

Introduction

Soap Carving For Children of All Ages introduced some basic techniques to soap carving. It focused on carving single bars of Ivory™ Soap using easily hand-made wooden carving tools to create both animate and inanimate objects. However, the one-inch thick Ivory bar limits the kind of things or animals one can carve.

In this book, we will expand the creative possibilities of soap carving by gluing bars of soap together to create a thicker carving medium. The main objective is to present some techniques of multiple soap bar carving of selected well-known North American mammals. A number of the groups I selected face a precarious existence and a hazardous future of further decline in population to the point of extirpation. I hope that this book will give you ideas on using the techniques described to come up with your own exciting patterns and carvings and to spur you to learn about the natural history of animals you plan to carve. In addition, the patterns can also be transferred to soft wood, such as basswood, to introduce you to wood carving.

The basic format will include some comments on natural history and wildlife conservation, a reading list of books with fine reference photographs, and a listing of techniques that can be applied to carving other animals. For example, how to add whiskers on animals is described in the carving of the Harp Seal; this technique can be used to insert whiskers on other mammals, such as an African lion, manatee, or walrus. Additional readings have been included because they have excellent photographs of the actual live animals and natural history information about the animal to be carved. This will be followed by the step-by-step carving process.

Contents

Chapter One: Some Techniques and Tips

Ivory Soap™

Traditional Ivory Soap™ will be used exclusively in this book. Ivory Moisture Care™ is not recommended as that soap is more expensive and does not have the right consistency for carving. Fresh bars of soap should always be used as old bars become brittle, shatter easily, and hard to carve. Also I have been told that persons using different kinds of cosmetic soaps for carving have experienced allergic responses, apparently due to the various aromatic and other compounds incorporated into the soaps' formulations.

needs. However, it is not essential to have or use steel tools to carve the animals in this book.

It should be emphasized, however, that when carving soap, the carving tools , whether they are made of steel or wood, need to be cleaned frequently to remove the buildup of soap on the cutting edges. The woodcarver does not experience this problem very often unless carving a wood that has a lot of gummy material, such as pitch, embedded in the wood grain.

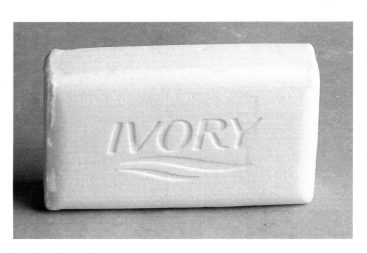

Ivory™ Soap Bar.

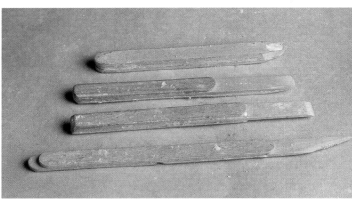

Four wooden carving tools made from popsicle sticks (craft sticks). Top to bottom: deep gouge, shallow gouge, chisel, skew blade.

Wooden Carving Tools

In my previous book I described the step-wise process of making wooden carving tools with readily available materials and tools. I used wooden knives primarily as a safety factor and as an inexpensive alternative to purchasing metal tools and knives. Special shapes could be made quickly and inexpensively to meet special needs of a particular carving.

In this book I intersperse the use of steel carving tools in my carvings, as they are particularly suitable for the initial roughing-out stages of the carvings. They cut more smoothly than wooden tools. Steel carving tools should not be as sharp as is needed in woodcarving, as soap is a soft, well-lubricated medium allowing for easy smooth cuts. Steel carving tools come in different shapes such as the chisel, skew (an angled cutting-edged chisel), gouge (curved cutting edge), v-shaped, or various knife-shaped tools to meet specific carving

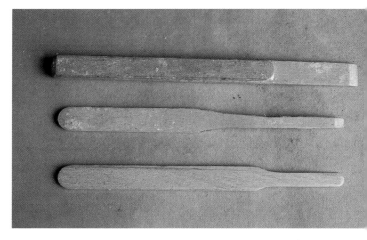

Special shapes can be made easily. This photo shows, from top to bottom, a standard size chisel, a narrow-width chisel and a tapered round-edged scraper. The narrow chisel is needed to carve in tight areas, such as between the legs of animals, and, in particular, on a one-piece carving where the animal and base are made out of the same Ivory soap bar. The tapered round-edged scraper is used for fine detailing such as outlining eyes or scoring fur.

The disadvantages of wooden tools are that they need to be sharpened frequently by stropping them across 400 grit wet/dry sandpaper and that they do not cut as smoothly as steel blades.

Additional Tools

A straight edged scraper is an essential tool to remove the Ivory logo from the soap bar, to produce flat surfaces on soap bars to be joined together in multiple bar carvings.

Steel Carving Tools

Shown, from left to right, are some steel carving tools: a potato peeler, curved blade knife, a straight-edged knife, and a skew-shaped knife. The different shapes of the cutting edges permit the carver to make different shaped cuts to meet specific needs.

A scraper can be made out of wood or metal. It can be made out of a thin piece of hardwood or metal (approximately 6" by ½" by 3/16"). It can also be made by gluing two Popsicle sticks together. Sand the edges smooth by holding them vertically and moving the scraper back and forth against the flat surface of the sandpaper.

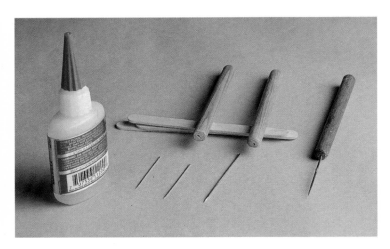

Straight calipers and a ruler with a depth gauge are needed tools.

Adhesives

Dissecting needles are made out of different-sized sewing needles that do not readily bend, or from a safety pin's straight sharp portion. This tool may be used in many ways to add fine details to the carving, such as outlines around the eyes and nose. It is made by drilling an appropriate size hole in the end of a 0.25" (1/4") four-inch length wooden dowel, inserting the blunt end of the needle into the dowel and gluing.

Several different kinds of adhesives can be used to glue soap together. From left to right are melded Ivory soap, SuperGlue (cyanoacrylate), sticky craft glue, and sodium silicate. SuperGlue and the craft glue are fine for gluing a carving to a base after it has been completed. SuperGlue dries and hardens very quickly to a brittle consistency. Sodium silicate has been used in years past, dries to a brittle consistency, but is probably difficult to find today.

Ivory Soap Adhesive

Melded Ivory soap pieces appear to be the best all-around adhesive. After application and drying, the soap adhesive welds the soap together as it is essentially the same material as the carved material. After drying, SuperGlue and sodium silicate become hard, brittle and brownish in color. It is difficult to carve through the hardened SuperGlue and sodium silicate, as any slip will damage the softer soap. Craft glue dries to a rubbery whitish consistency.

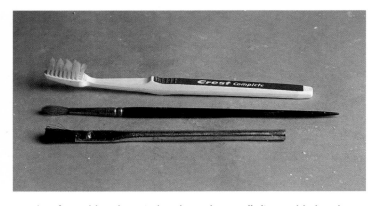

A soft toothbrush, paintbrush, and a small disposable brush are essential tools needed to clean the soap debris from the carving.

Joining Soap Bars

Place some pieces of Ivory Soap on a flat plate ; add a little water and mix together to form a thick soap slurry.

Place the scraped flat surfaces of the Ivory Soap bars on the wet slurry. Add a few more drops of water if it appears to be too thick. The bars of soap will melt slightly from the wet slurry.

Left: After scraping the soap bar to remove the logo, gently rub the two bars together to match the two surfaces as closely as possible.

After a minute or so press the two bars together at their wet surfaces, and gently squeeze the bars together and hold for thirty seconds to a minute.

While holding the two bars together, gently rub some of the soap slurry where the bars are joined together. Make additional slurry as needed.

Soap can also be melded by placing Ivory Soap pieces in a small Pyrex™ bowl. Add a little bit of water (a teaspoon or so) to the soap pieces. Place the bowl into a sauce pan with water, and boil. Stir occasionally. *Care must be taken not to get burned.*

After the soap has dried, from several hours to overnight, scrape the edge of the joined parts to make them smooth.

The joined bars, after being scraped smooth.

Heat and stir until the soap chunks dissolve into an even consistency. After it has cooled, transfer the melded soap into a small bottle. It is now ready for use. After storage, you can heat the soap in a sauce pan with hot water before using. The consistency of the melded soap will be slightly softer than the original state of the soap.

Repairing Breaks

Accidental breaks in soap carving are facts of life. However, most can be repaired. Put melded soap on the surface of the broken end. Then carefully attaching the broken piece to the body. After the glue dries, it can be carved. Do not use any other glue if you wish to detail the carving further.

Broken ear pinna is shown from the bear cub climbing a tree trunk.

Broken ear lobe is being glued using melded glue.

Mortise and Tenon Joint

The woodworker's mortise and tenon joint is described here for use in soap carving. A mortise is a rectangular flat cavity cut into material such as wood. The tenon is that portion of another material that is sized to fit snugly into the cavity or mortise. In this type of joint the tenon fits at right angle into the mortise. Beyond serving as a method for joining two pieces, for soap carving this joint is modified by carving and both become part of the carved animal.

A mortise is formed by carving in a rectangular groove in the large surface of one soap bar. The size is determined by the size of the small end dimensions of the second soap bar, which will serve as the tenon.

The tenon (the second soap bar) is then inserted at a right angle in the mortise after melded glue is placed in the mortise. By gently squeezing the mortise and tenon together, and allowing to dry overnight, a strong weld will be formed. The soap bars, so joined, now make a carving block.

Chapter Two: Harp Seal

Special Techniques

1. Carving an in-the-round animal
2. Making surfaces smooth using a damp paper towel
3. Attaching vibrissae (whiskers on snout)
4. Making a base using two fused Ivory Soap bars

We will start with a beautiful subject to carve, the newborn Harp Seal, also called the Greenland or Saddleback Seal. They are unique as they are born with a white silky fur. They begin to moult starting about a week after birth and moulting is completed by three to four weeks of age. They make a superb subject for carving with white Ivory Soap. Their large black eyes make them even more striking as a carving subject.

During the period that they are in the white phase, they are hunted for their white fur. The Harp Seal is found in Eastern Canada along the St. Lawrence River basin and northward in the open Arctic Atlantic Ocean. They are distributed further in the Arctic region of Europe and Asia.

Additional Reading

King, Judith. *Seals of the World.* Comstock Pub. Assoc. Ithaca, NY. 1983.
Switzer, Merebeth. *Nature's Children SEALS* Grolier Educational Corp. Danbury, CT. 1986.

Carving the Harp Seal

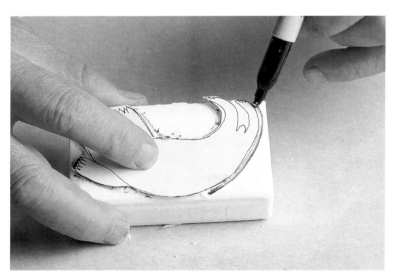

First scrape off the logo of the Ivory Soap bar. Outline the top view pattern on the bar with a pencil or sharp pointed instrument, such as a dissecting needle. I am using a Sharpie™ to make the outline more visible to the reader.

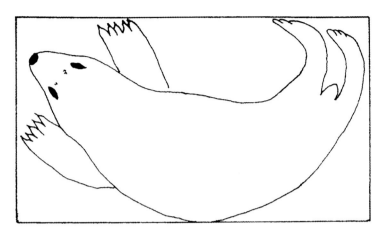

Top view.

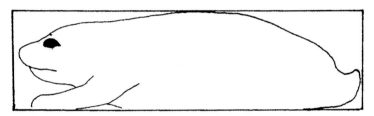

Lateral view of left side.

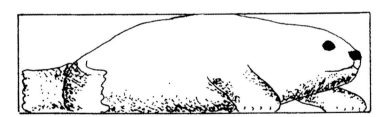

Lateral view of right side.

Hind flippers (above) and front flippers (below).

Frontal view.

Frontal view of head.

Continue cutting all the way through the bar along the body's outline.

Make stop cuts on the outline using a straight, sharp-pointed blade.

Start carving the outline of the head and flippers.

Make horizontal cuts to remove the soap to the stop cuts.

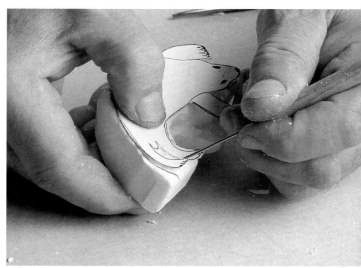

Use a dissecting needle to start separating the right and left hind flippers.

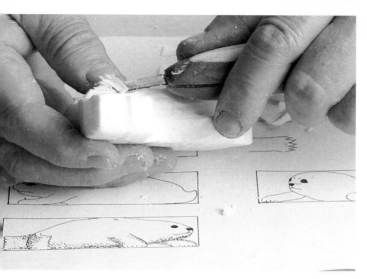

Shape the hind flippers to obtain their approximate widths.

Carve the front flippers so that they will be in a downward (ventral) direction.

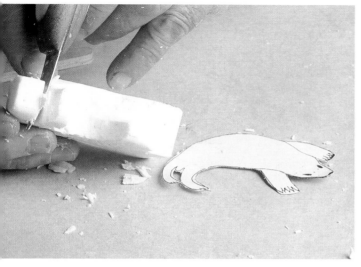

Carefully remove soap between the flippers to further shape them.

Further shape the area between the head area and the flippers.

Turn the carving over to show the abdominal surface, and begin to differentiate the front flippers from the head. A second carving in a more advanced stage is shown for comparison.

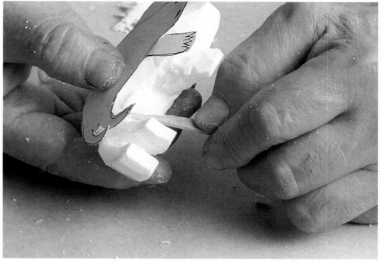

Place the pattern on top of the carving and further shape the body outline.

Carefully shape the upper part (dorsal) of the front flippers so that the paw portion will be lower.

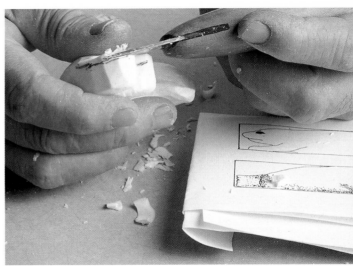

Rough out the approximate height of the head.

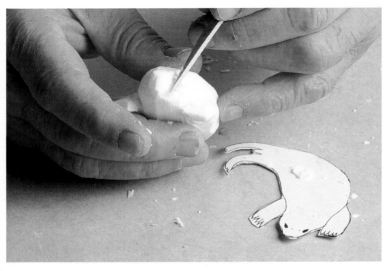

Roughly shape the sides of the head.

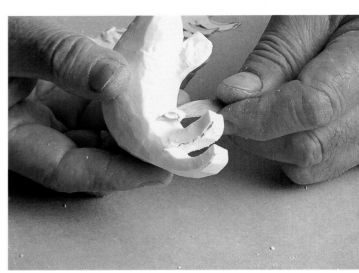

Continue shaping the body.

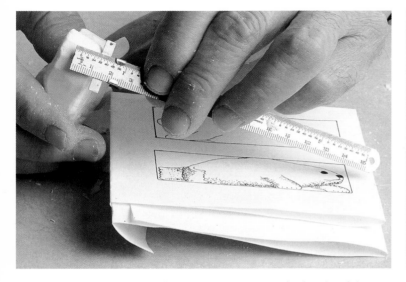

Use a ruler or a pair of calipers to determine the height of the head. Some sort of measuring device should be used throughout the carving process.

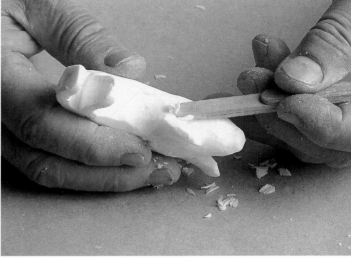

Shape the junctions between the front flippers and the body using a gouge.

Further shape the hind flippers with a straight narrow-pointed knife.

A side view (lateral) of the carving.

Shape the head by carefully scraping with a straight narrow-pointed knife.

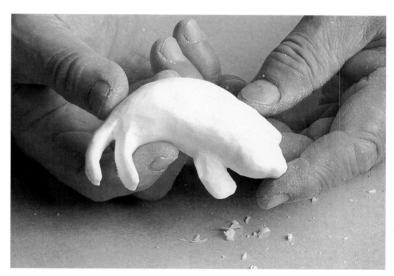

A top view (dorsal) of the carving.

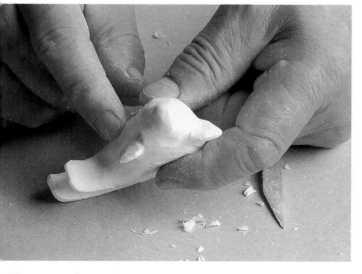

The carving from a frontal view at this stage.

A bottom view (ventral) of the carving.

Scrape smooth the transition between the flippers and the body.

Carefully scrape the hind flippers to form the definitive shapes.

Shape the undersurface (ventral) of the front flippers.

Carefully carve the ends of the hind flippers so that the marginal digits will be longer than the central digits.

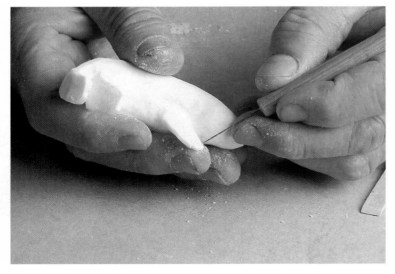

Make four grooves using a dissecting needle to indicate the separation of the five digits on the flipper.

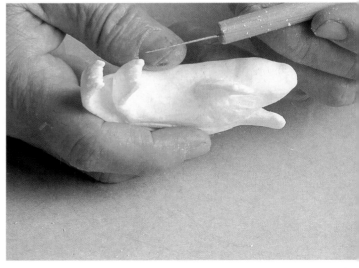

Use the dissecting needle to make grooves to represent the skin between the hind digits.

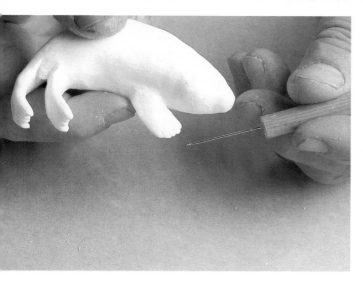

The appearance of the detailed front and hind flippers.

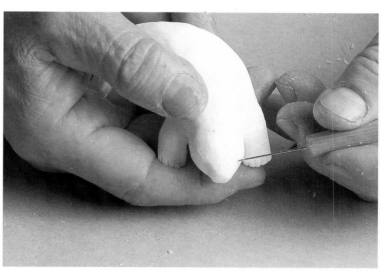

Outline the eyes using the dissecting needle.

Detail the undersurface of the head.

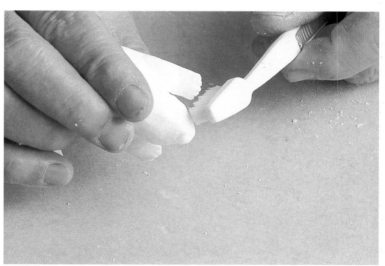

Brush away soap particles using a soft toothbrush.

Outline the mouth and nostrils using a dissecting needle.

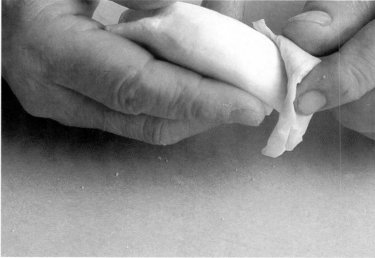

Smooth the animal's surface by gently rubbing with a slightly dampened paper towel. Remember that water will dissolve soap, so use the dampened towel with discretion.

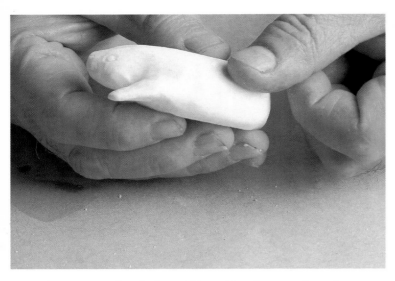

Appearance of seal after rubbing with a dampened towel

Paint the grooves between the toes on the front paws.

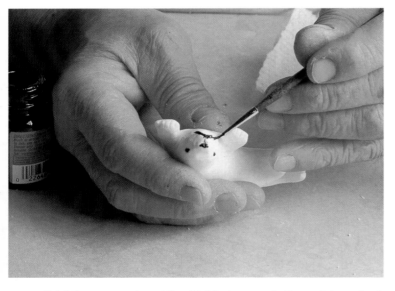

Paint the eyes and nostrils with black enamel. Also paint a pair of small black spots between the eyes as shown in adjacent photograph to the right.

Cut some bristles from a disposable paint brush to prepare for attaching vibrissae. You can also use an old hair brush made out of hog bristles. I prefer using hog bristles because the hair diameters vary and I can select the individual hairs that I want to use.

Make tiny holes using your fine dissecting needle where the vibrissae on the snout are located. (I forgot to use a needle and am using one of my fine-pointed tweezers in this photograph.) Hairs will be inserted into the holes.

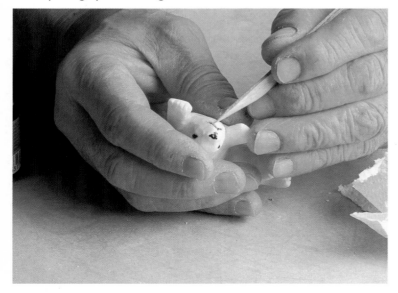

Carefully scrape away excess paint around eyes and nostrils.

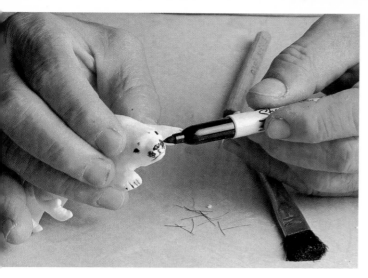

Blacken the holes with black enamel or a fine black felt tip pen (e.g. Sharpie™) so that they can be located easily.

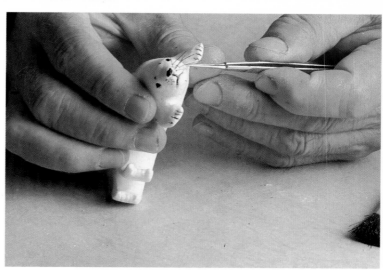

Pick up a hair with a fine pair of tweezers and carefully insert into one of the holes previously made.

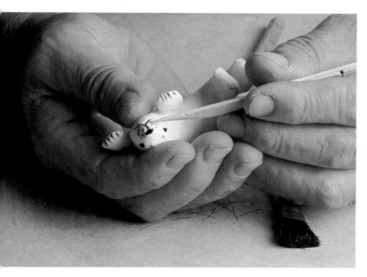

Scrape away the excess black, and the black holes become visible.

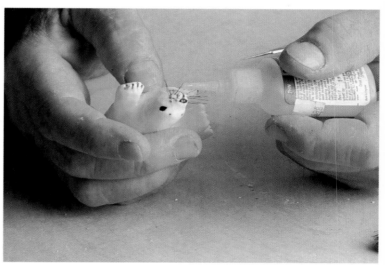

Carefully glue the hairs at the attachment points using a thin SuperGlue (cyanoacrylate glue).

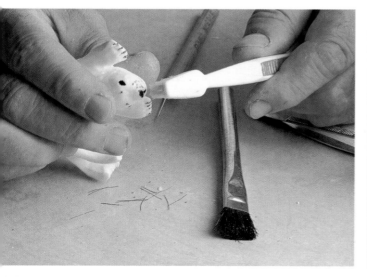

Clean the snout using a soft brush.

To make an "ice floe" base out of two Ivory Soap bars, first remove the logos and scrape the edges to be joined straight and even.

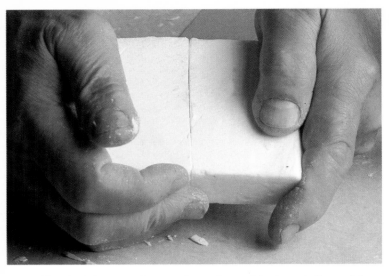

Test the joint to make sure the surface of the base is flat and the joint is fairly tight.

Place the carved seal temporarily on the soap bar "ice floe", and outline an irregular shape on the base.

The bars are glued together using a SuperGlue. The bars can also be glued together using other methods described in the introductory chapter.

A slurry of Ivory Soap (making it is described in the introductory chapter) is rubbed into the visible joint spaces after the bars were glued together and held tightly together for several minutes.. They should be allowed to dry overnight. After drying, the surface will be scraped to simulate an "ice floe".

The harp seal is glued on to the base using SuperGlue after carving the desired shape of the base. Score in irregularities on the base to further simulate the ice floe.

Harp Seal on ice floe

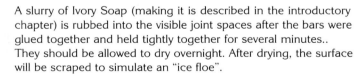

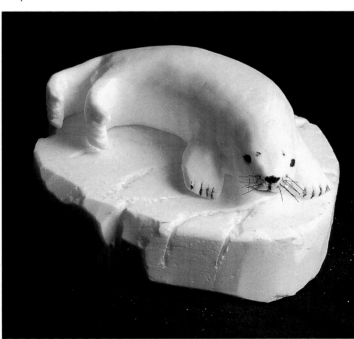

Chapter Three: Black-Tailed Prairie Dog

Special Technique

Carving an in-the-round carving using two Ivory soap bars joined together.

The prairie dog is a roly-poly vegetarian with short legs found in the central prairie states. Unlike the Harp seal, otter, wolf, or bear, they are not found in any other continent, so they are truly a North American native. They live in communities called prairie dog towns. Their short extremities do not allow them to make fast long sprints to avoid predators. They are seen next to their burrows, into which they can scurry and get away from predators such as hawks and coyotes. There are several species and subspecies of prairie dogs but the black-tailed prairie dog is the most widely distributed.

It is most unfortunate that with significant loss of habitat, human eradication efforts, and disease, prairie dogs are now severely depleted in numbers. To me the prairie dog is a fine representative of a mammal inhab-iting the prairie states, together with the fact that it is truly a native of this continent, and that is why I selected it.. In addition, it makes an excellent subject for carving two Ivory soap bars glued together.

Readings

Casey, Denise. *The Friendly Prairie Dog*. G.P. Putmam's and Sons. New York, N.Y. Photos by Dr. T.W. Clark. 1990.

Chace, G.E. *Wonders of Prairie Dogs*. Dodd, Mead and Company, New York. 1976.

Hirschi, Ron. *Where are my Prairie Dogs and Black-footed Ferrets?* Bantam Books, New York, N.Y. Photos by Erwin and Peggy Bauer. 1992.

Lottridge, C.B. and S. Horner. *Nature's Children PRAIRIE DOGS*. Grolier Educational Corp. Danbury, CT. 1986.

Carving the Prairie Dog

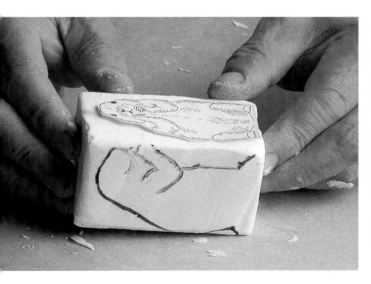

The fusion of two Ivory soap bars was described in Chapter One. Outline the patterns on the block, using a marking device such as a dissecting needle or pencil.

Rough out the side profile of the Prairie dog.

Pattern found on following page.

Side view.

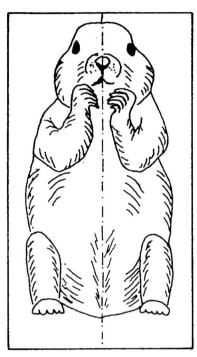

Front view.

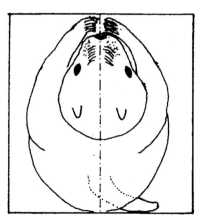

Top view.

Outline the front profile again.

Rough out the front profile of the Prairie dog.

Rough out the tail.

Make shallow stop cuts to outline the front legs and start shaping the body.

Start shaping the head.

Rough out the front legs and separate them from the head.

Rough out the thighs, making them identifiable from the body.

Side view of the carving

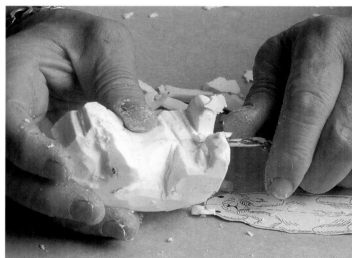

Carve between the hind legs.

Front view of the carving

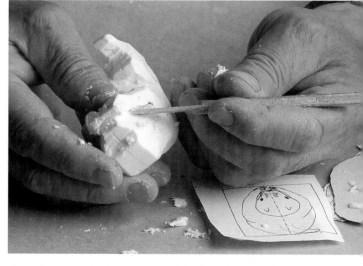

Carve between the front legs and the head, separating them.

Shape the head and neck so that they begin to have curved surfaces.

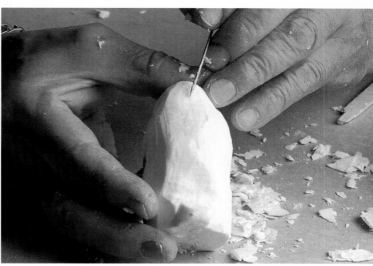

Appearance of back after the joint has been filled.

Shape the body, giving it a roundish appearance.

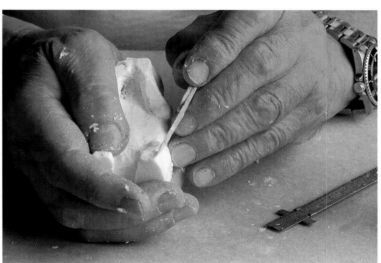

Shape the hind legs.

The needle is pointing to the joint line between the two soap bars. Fill it with melded soap.

Side view of carving at this stage.

Front view of carving at this stage.

Detail the neck area, making the head distinguishable from the body.

Locate the positions of the eyes evenly using a measuring device such as a ruler or a pair of calipers.

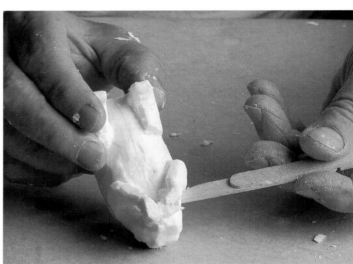

Detail the front legs.

Carefully detail the outlines of the eyes.

Detail the front paws.

Brush the carving again

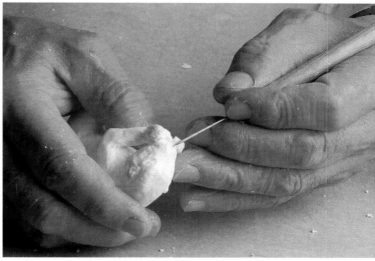

Outline the nostrils and add grooves to the front paws, using the dissecting needle.

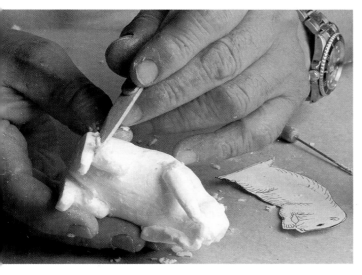

Further detail the hind legs.

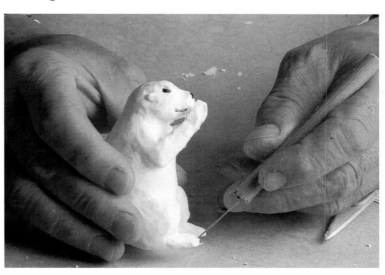

Make grooves between the toes using the dissecting needle.

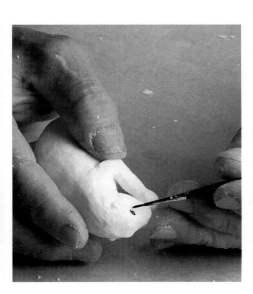

Paint the eyes black with quick drying enamel.

Oblique side view of Prairie Dog carving.

Oblique frontal view of Prairie Dog carving.

Chapter Four: River Otter

Special Technique

Joining two soap bars with mortise and tenon joint where both the mortise and tenon are integral parts of the animal.

Two different genera of otters are found in North America, the sea otters and river otters. Other species of otters are found throughout the world. Sea otters are located along the Western coastal shores of North America and extend across the ocean to Japan. Their numbers have decreased significantly due to pollution, disease and other factors.. They are popular tourist attractions as free wild animals, particularly along a 200-mile stretch from California's Monterey Bay region southward.

River otters were once widely distributed in the United States and Southern Canada and common up to a 100 years ago. With destruction of their wetlands habitats, intense hunting for their fur, and in more recent years, the unintentional poisoning through pesticides and toxic wastes, they were decimated or eliminated in a great deal of their former locations. With elimination of hunting, and through restoration and relocation projects, they are making a comeback. They are now found more commonly in the West Coast, Southeastern states, and Great Lakes region. They are popular attractions at theme parks. There is a species of giant river otter found in South America. This species is also facing significant decrease in numbers.

River otters are short-legged truly aquatic mammals, which have webbed feet and strong cylindrical tails (about 65% of the body). The sea otters are larger, have large hind legs, and have shorter tails comprising about 25% of the body length. The river otters make their homes in the banks of streams. They feed primarily on fish, amphibians and crayfish.

This chapter will illustrate the step-by-step process for carving a standing river otter. Since the otter has a long body with a long tail, it presents problems in terms of making designs that maximize the carving size using Ivory soap. My solution was to design a standing River Otter. The vertically placed tenon becomes most of the otter while part of the mortise is carved away, leaving a portion to become the otter's tail. The exposed lowest part of the tenon is carved and becomes the terminal portions of the animal's extremities.

Readings

Cousteau Society. *Otters*. Little Simon Publishing by Simon and Schuster. New York, N.Y. 1993.

Gingerich, J.L. *Florida's Fabulous Mammals*. World Publications, Tampa, FL 1994

Paine, Stefani. *The World of the SEA OTTER*. Sierra Book Club. San Francisco, CA. Photographs by Jeff Foott. 1995.

Virginia, B and R.A. Silverstein. *The Sea Otter*. Milbrook Press. Milbrook, MA. 1995.

Carving the River Otter

Place vertically oriented Ivory Soap tenon near one end of the flat surface of the Ivory Soap mortise. Mark the outline of the tenon on the mortise location.

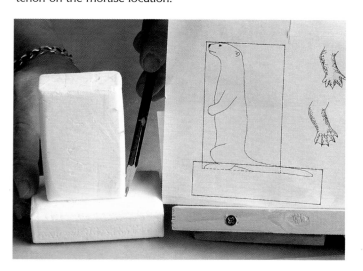

Make a shallow stop cut on the marked line indicating the margin of the mortise.

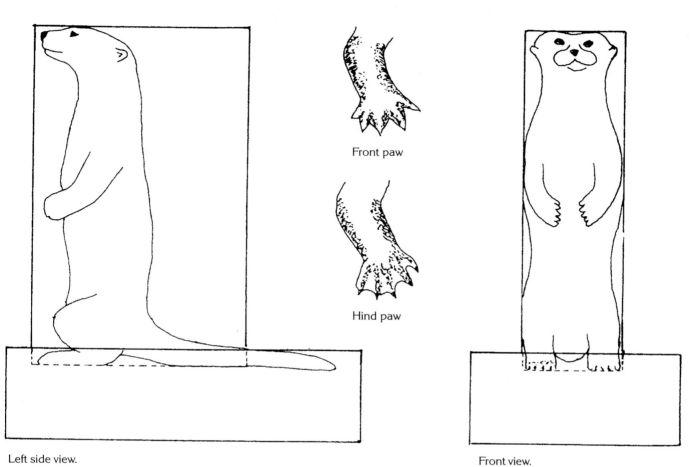

Front paw

Hind paw

Left side view.

Front view.

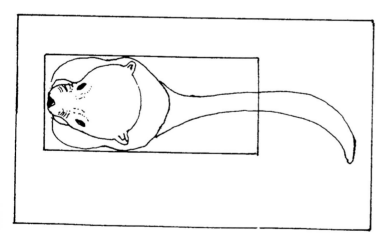

Top view.

Remove the soap within the marked lines using a chisel to make the mortise.

The necessary flat surface of the groove is attained by using a chisel to scrape the groove.

Place the tenon in the mortise slot and test it for fit. If it does not fit, make another line around the tenon and cut away the soap in the mortise along the line. Repeat until the tenon fits tightly into the mortise.

Measure the height of the tenon to make sure that it is in deep enough in the mortise.

Use a gauge or ruler to measure the depth of the groove. The depth should be about 3/16" deep, with the walls of the groove as close to a right angle as is possible.

Place glue in mortise and insert tenon. You may use other adhesives described in Chapter One.

The gaps in the joint line are filled with either melded soap or fine pieces of Ivory waste pressed into the gaps.

Outline the location of the tail on the mortise portion of the carving.

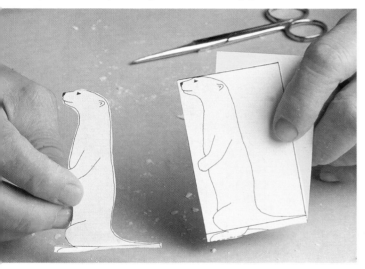

The side pattern is reinforced with a backing, and cut out. The bottom portion is bent at a right angle. The bent portion will be the part of the otter located in the mortise.

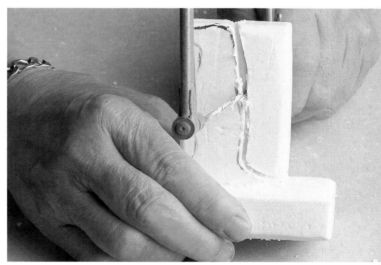

Saw the back (dorsal) outline of the otter with a Coping saw. The lower back part of the carving will include a portion of the tail coming out of the body. If you do not have a Coping saw you can carve it with a knife.

Transfer the pattern on to the Ivory Soap. Make sure that the bottom bent portion of the pattern is not included in the transfer.

Carve the front (ventral) profile of the otter, and mark the approximate positions of the front legs.

Make a center line on the back. Outline the front and hind legs, and the tail.

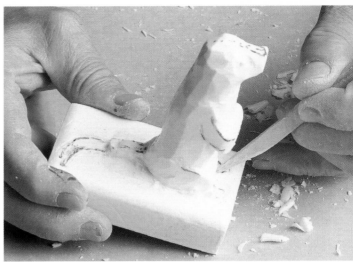

The hind legs located in the mortise area can now be carved.

Carve the body to start delineating the front and hind legs.

Make shallow horizontal cuts about an eighth of an inch deep all around the otter, making sure that the tail and tenon portion of the soap bar are not removed. The final depth of 3/16" will be achieved in the final stages by scraping the base. A straight blade or chisel is used for most of this part of the carving. A skew blade and gouge should be used in the tail area.

This photograph shows the side profile after the base was lowered. This photo shows the tail in its entirety.

Make shallow stop cuts outlining the portion of the tail located on the base.

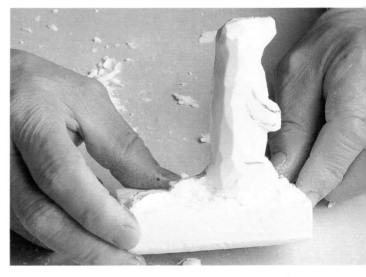

Use a measuring device to compare the carving with the pattern before shaping the head and neck. *Be sure to leave enough material on the head to carve out the ears.*

Shape and contour the hind legs.

Shape the front legs so that the paws appear to be holding something.

Lightly groove the spaces between the toes on the hind legs using a dissecting needle.

Detail the front paws using a dissecting needle to lightly score the spaces between the digits.

Shape the tail so that the visible part is roundish and be sure that there is a smooth transition on the tail at the joint between the two soap bars.

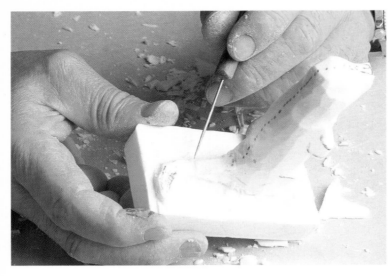

The dissecting needle is pointing to the joint line on the tail. Fill in the joint as needed where the tenon meets the perimeter of the mortise with melded Ivory Soap, and smooth the joint line with the tip of your forefinger.

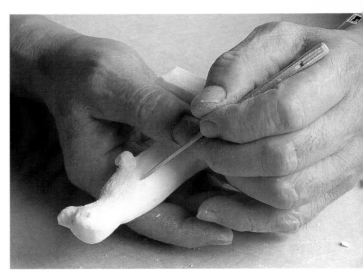

The fur may be lightly scored on the body. The technique for simulating fur is described and illustrated in Chapter Five, on the Wolf.

Scrape the body so that it will have a roundish contour by scraping the soap with a straight blade.

Contour the snout.

Carefully locate and carve the outlines of the ears.

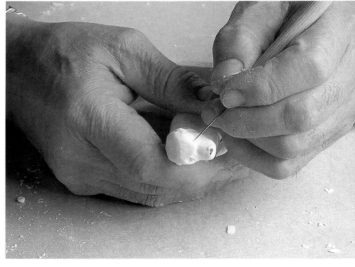

Outline the eyes, using a dissecting needle.

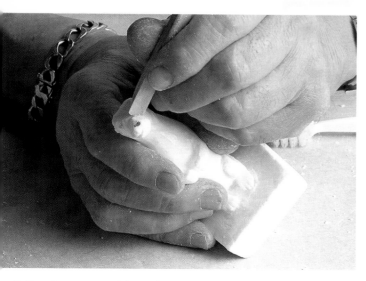

Refine the snout and face after the eyes have been outlined.

Side view of standing River Otter.

The eyes and nostrils are painted black and the excess carefully scraped off..

Front view of standing River Otter.

Vibrissae are attached and trimmed. The technique of attaching whiskers is described in Chapter Two, on the Harp Seal.

Chapter Five: Wolf

Special Techniques

Simulating fur
Undercutting

Wolves have been vilified, loved, and admired, both in stories and in reality. They belong to the canine family, which includes coyotes, foxes, and domestic dogs. There are several species of wolves in North America: the Timber wolf, Gray wolf, and Red wolf. In the lower 48 states they are on the endangered list of species and found in the wild only in small, isolated populations in different parts. Wolves are still holding their own population-wise in Canada and Alaska.

I recently recalled a painting that hung in my parents' home I used to see as a child growing up in Alaska. The painting was an eerie night scene of a wolf sitting on its hindquarters howling towards the night sky. That may have been a subconscious reason why I selected the wolf for inclusion in this book. My fascination for howling canines also stems from the times I visited municipal zoos and started howling like a wolf while standing in front of their cages.. Within a few minutes I had the all of the wolves and coyotes howling in unison, much to the chagrin of the zoo-keepers, I am sure.

I designed the Wolf to be sitting on a base because the carver will have less breakage problems compared to a wolf standing on all four legs. However, it is a bit more difficult to carve because of the undercuts that have to be made between the legs , body and base. A method of overcoming that problem will be described. In addition, a method of simulating fur will be described.

Readings

Ross, Judy. *Nature's Children WOLVES* Grolier Educational Corp. Danbury,CT. 1986.
Patent, D.H. and W. Muñoz. *Gray Wolf Red Wolf*. Clarion Books, New York. 1990.

Carving the Wolf

The wolf requires a mortise and tenon joint. The process was described in carving the River Otter. The only difference is the different placement of the tenon on the mortise.

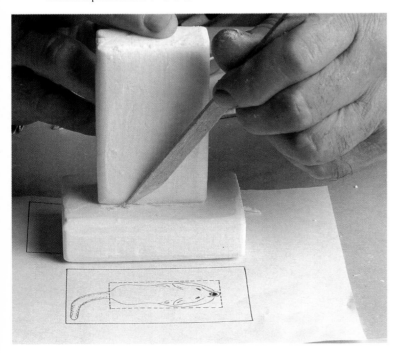

Melded glue is placed in the mortise.

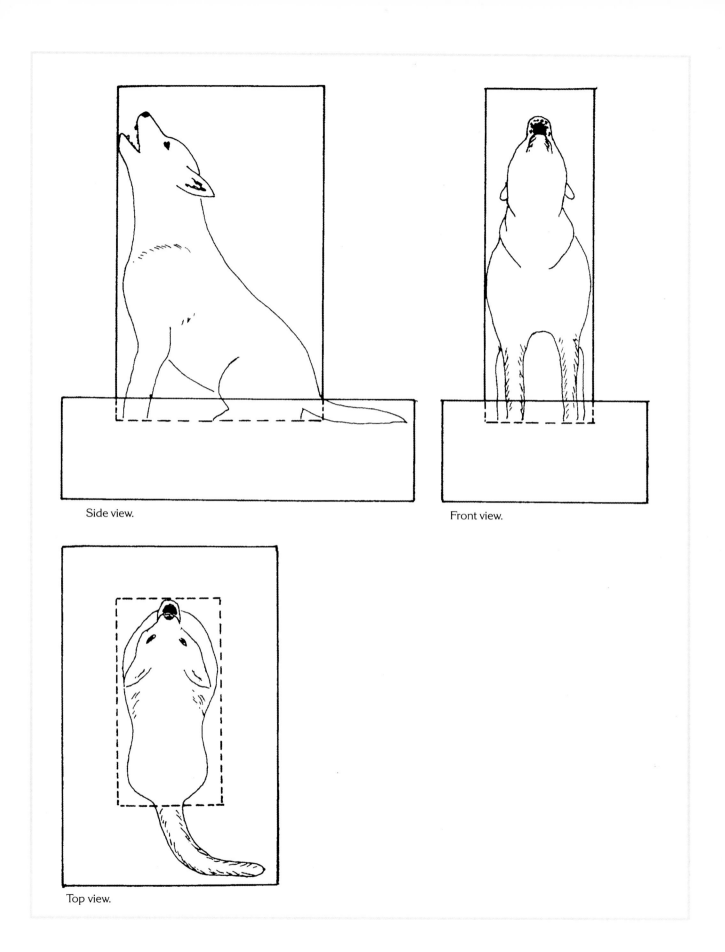

Side view.

Front view.

Top view.

The side pattern outline with the bottom folded over is transferred to the Ivory Soap, as described in the River Otter. Don't forget to *outline the tail* on the mortise portion of the Ivory Soap.

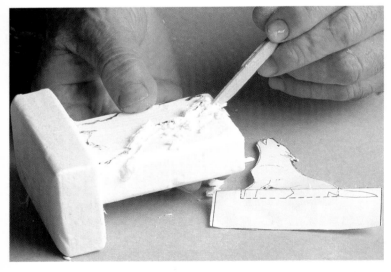

Stop cuts are made outlining the wolf, using a sharp-pointed straight blade. A coping saw was used for this step in the carving of the River Otter.

Soap is carved away to the stop cuts. The stop cuts and removal of unwanted soap can be repeated.

The remaining unwanted soap is removed by carving.

The front portion of the outlined pattern is carved.

38

Stop cuts are made outlining the previously marked tail located on the mortise part of the soap.

Carefully carve the ears to delineate them.

Remove the surface of the mortise portion in the area around the tail to a depth of approximately 1/8" depth. The tail is seen next to the knife in this photograph. Unlike the River Otter, the base of the tail is located at the junction of the tenon and mortise.

Start carving the outline of the open mouth using a narrow blade knife.

Start shaping the sides of the head after outlining the head, ears, and body from the back surface.

Rough out the neck and begin to shape the rest of the body.

Continue removing the surface surrounding the rest of the mortise area to a depth of 1/8" so that the ground level parts of the legs of the wolf (which are parts of the vertical tenon) are exposed.

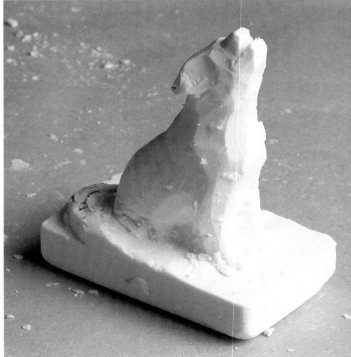

The wolf at this stage of the carving.

Carefully begin to remove material under the abdomen and behind the front legs using a sharp-pointed straight blade. Repeat carving from the other side until the underparts of the abdomen are exposed.

Carefully carve out the space between the front legs.

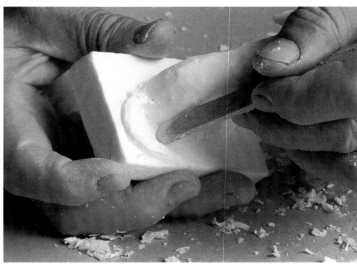

Use a shallow gouge to help shape the tail to a roundish configuration. Then use a chisel to flatten the surface surrounding the tail.

Use a long narrow chisel tool to reach into the rear portions of the carving, particularly the part between the hind quarters and inner surfaces of the hind quarters. Shape the hind and front legs and the body.

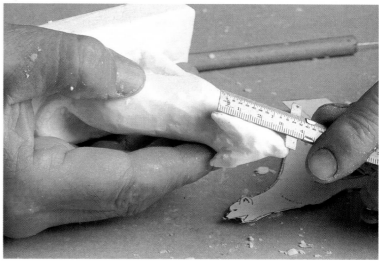

Use a ruler to make sure that both ears are the same size and are located evenly on both sides. Their positions and sizes are corrected by carving.

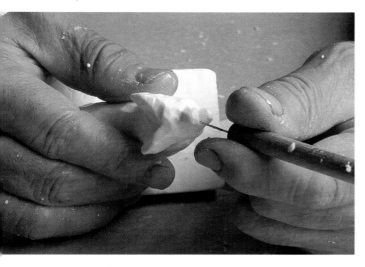

Deepen the mouth cavity using a dissecting needle. A tongue can be delineated by this method. However, I have not attempted to carve teeth.

The inner surfaces of the ear pinnae are carved to make curved surfaces, using a narrow rounded-edged gouge.

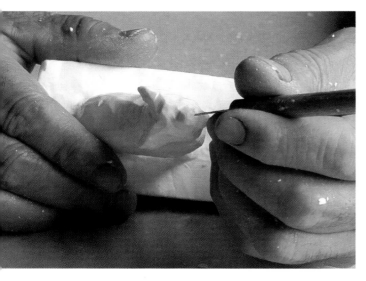

The nostrils are outlined using a dissecting needle.

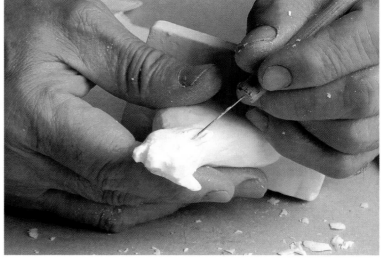

The external ear canals (external auditory meati) are deepened, using a dissecting needle.

Outline the eyes using the dissecting needles.

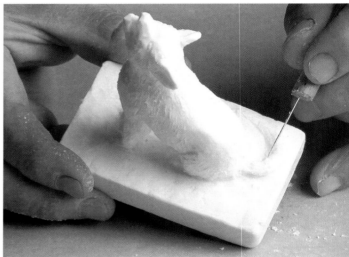

Brush away the etched soap debris, and look for areas that may have been missed. Repeat the etching and cleaning as needed.

The carving at this stage.

Fur is simulated by using a dissecting needle to etch the carving. To be more accurate, the directions of hair tracts can be determined by looking at photographs of wolves in books listed at the beginning of this chapter.

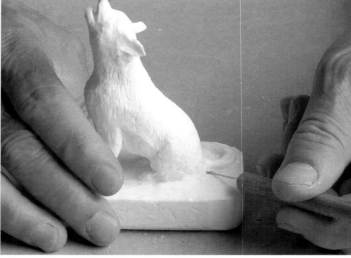

The tail is etched to simulate hair.

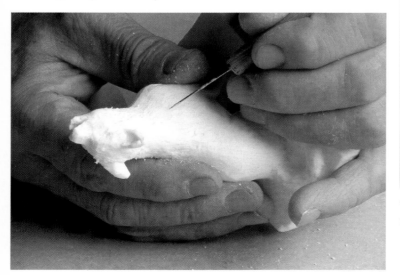

The area under the base of the tail is undercut to open up space under the base of the tail.

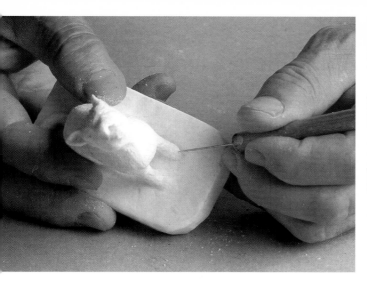

The paws are detailed, and the spaces between digits grooved with a dissecting needle.

Side (lateral) view of the Wolf.

The sharp corners are rounded off to soften the appearance of the base.

Front (ventral) view of the Wolf.

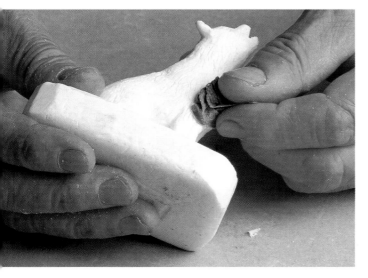

Fine debris from the etching process is wiped off using a slightly dampened towel. This process removes most of the remaining debris that stuck to the carving after brushing.

Back (dorsal) view of the Wolf.

43

Chapter Six: Black Bear- *The Spirit Bear*

Special Technique

Carving an in-the-round animal and base as a single piece using two fused bars of Ivory soap.

Bears are widely distributed in North America with three basic species: the Polar bear, Brown bear, and Black bear. The white Polar bear is found in the Northern latitudes of Canada and Alaska. The huge Brown bear, or Grizzly, has gained a reputation for its ferocious behavior. They are found mostly in Alaska and Canada. In an effort to reestablish them in the lower 48 United States, some have been transplanted to Yellowstone National Park in Wyoming.

The smaller black bear is more widely distributed than the other bears in parts of North America, although their range and numbers have been reduced because of the loss of habitat. In some regions, they have increased in numbers and become nuisances, where they invade rural and urban areas, damaging homes and community garbage dumps. The black bear may have fur varying in color from black to brown, to white. The latter, called the *Spirit Bear,* is found in pristine rainforests on several isolated islands in British Columbia, Canada. This is a unique race of black bears, as one in ten cubs is born white. Unfortunately its pristine forest is endangered by clear-cut logging, which not only destroys its unique habitat, but the home for other endangered species such as the Salmon, Grizzly, and both Bald and Golden Eagles. Black bears are unusual because they give birth to cubs while hibernating. The cubs suckle and grow while their mother continues hibernating. By spring, when the mother wakes up and starts foraging for food, they are big and strong enough to have a much better chance for survival.

I intend the Ivory soap carving to represent the white *Spirit Bear,* now that you know that there really is a *white* Black Bear.

Readings

Furtman, Michael. *Black Bear Country.* Northwood Press. Minnetonka, MN. 1998.

Greenland, Caroline. *Nature's Children POLAR BEARS.* Grolier Educational Corp. Danbury, CT. 1986.

Matthews, D and D. Guravich. *Polar Bear Cubs.* Simon and Schuster Books for Young Readers. New York. 1989

National Resources Defense Council. *Canadian Timber Company Targets Spirit Bear Habitat.* Nature's Voice March/April 2000.

Carving the Black Bear

The pattern is outlined on the double bars of fused Ivory soap. The method used to fuse the two soap bars is described in Chapter One.

Mark the position of the base around the entire soap carving and make a shallow stop cut along the marked line.

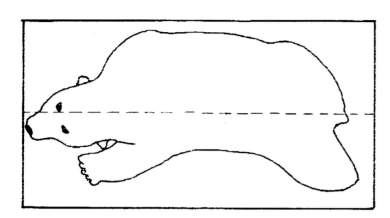

Top view.

Front view.

Left side view.

Right side view.

Make stop cuts outlining the top of the bear and carve to the stop cut, marking the position of the base.

Start carving under the abdomen, making sure that the base is kept intact. Do not worry about cutting all the way through the blocks at this time.

Rough out the underside of the head and parts of the forelegs, taking care to leave the base intact.

Start shaping the curves of the left side of the body.

Rough out the sides of the head and continue shaping the underside of the head and front of the forelegs.

Rough out the top side of the rear of the bear, including roughing out the general positions of the rear of the hind extremities.

Mark the locations of the legs on the right side of the carving and roughly round the body on that side.

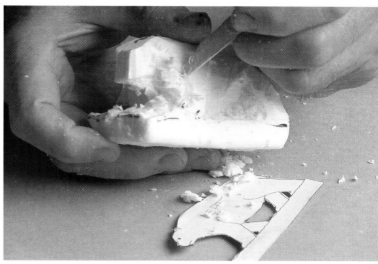

Rough out the curved shape of the left side of the body and the left front and rear extremities.

Noting the backward direction of the right front legs, undercut the abdomen to start rounding its undersurface.

Make a center line on the back surface of the curved body of the bear. Further rough out the hind part of the extremities. Take care not to remove the tail, which will be located at the most caudal portion of the center line.

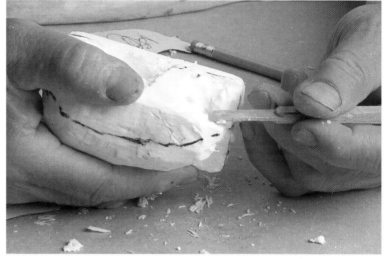

Carve an oversized general shape of the tail at the caudal end of the center line previously made. Do not undercut the tail at this time; just locate it for sizing and shaping later.

After locating the position of the ears using a pair of calipers, mark their positions.

Shape the sides of the bear.

Carve out an overly large general shape of the ears.

Frequently check your carving with the pattern, and shape accordingly.

Undercut the abdomen, making it round, and further shape the legs.

Now start sizing and shaping the tail.

Carefully undercut the abdomen from both sides and create an opening between the abdomen and the base.

Carve between the front legs using the narrow chisel, creating the space between the legs which connects to the previously-made opening.

Further shape the body to give it a roundish appearance.

Carve between the hind legs and connect that space with the opening in front of it.

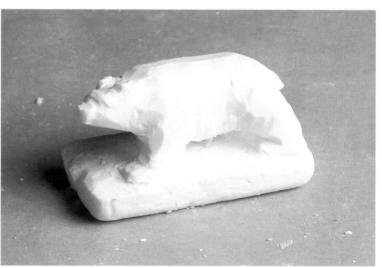

The left side of the bear at this stage of the carving.

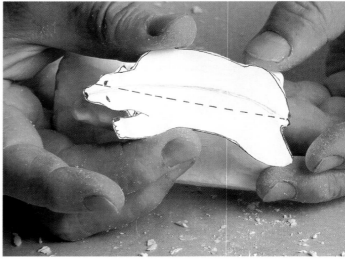

Check the general shape of the carving with the pattern.

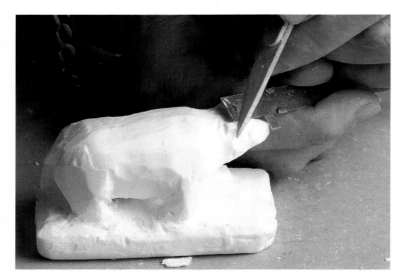

Measure the location of the ears on each side; size and shape them accordingly.

Refine the shapes of the front legs.

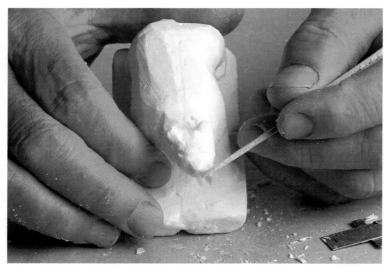

Shape the head and snout.

Refine the shapes of the hind legs and tail. Carefully undercut the tail so that the tip is free, and carve the tail with a roundish configuration.

Further refine the general shape of the ears.

Groove the spaces between the toes using a dissecting needle.

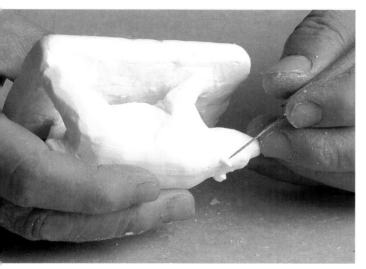

Carefully remove material from the outer ears to form concavities that will connect to the external ear canals.

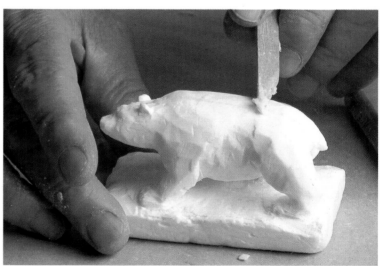

Refine the shape of the bear as necessary.

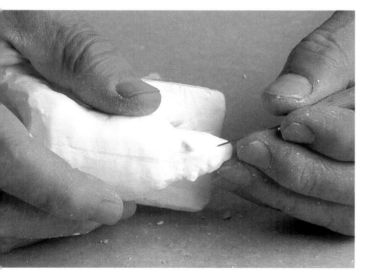

Outline the eyes and nostrils with a dissecting needle.

Simulate fur by making light parallel etches on the body using the dissecting needle.

The completed bear

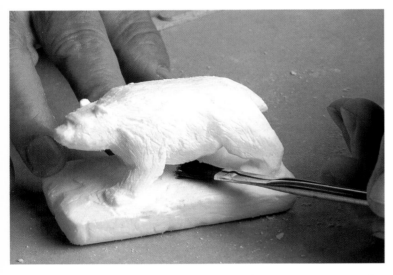

Clean with a brush, and repeat etching fur in missed areas, and cleaning as necessary.

Bear Cub Climbing a Tree

The bear cub climbing a tree is a carving made from four fused Ivory Soap bars. First two sets of double glued bars are made. Then one pair is glued at right angle to the second pair. One pair of bars makes the bear, while the second pair makes up the majority of the tree trunk. I found that it was more difficult to fit the legs of the bear cub carved by itself on to a carved tree trunk that was also carved separately than to carve the bear and tree trunk as a single entity.

Bear cub climbing a tree.

After painting the eyes, nostrils and mouth with black paint, scrape off the excess paint using a fine blade knife.

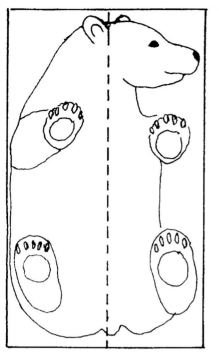

Undersurface (ventral) view.

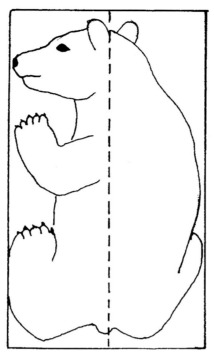

Oblique top (dorsal) view.

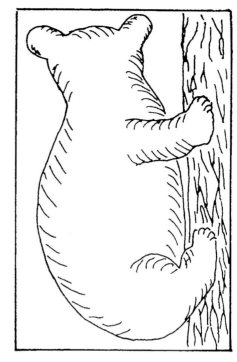

Right side view.

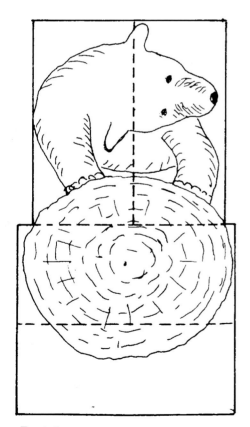

Front view.

Left side view.

Chapter Seven: Cougar
Carving by Lila Gilmer

Special Technique

"Wall-mount" style

Cougars, also called mountain lions, pumas, or panthers, are majestic big cats. At one time they were widely distributed throughout both North and South America, but because of loss of habitat and relentless hunting, they are no longer found in many parts of the Western Hemisphere. In order to preserve them, hunting them has been banned in many of the areas where they are still found. Florida has been making concerted efforts to preserve the separate race of wild Florida panthers. One such effort is the captive breeding program to increase their genetic variability because so few remain in the widely isolated areas of the State.

Cougars are efficient predators, with their short snouts and powerful jaws with strong teeth. Their paws with sharp claws are so powerful that they can kill prey with a single swipe. They are solitary animals that require large areas to survive, as they need to consume a large amount of prey such as deer, wild hogs, and rac-coons. However, they raise the ire of ranchers in the West, as they sometimes prey on cattle and sheep.

In this carving I have invited Lila Gilmer to carve the head and neck of a cougar using a double bar of Ivory Soap. Lila is a superb miniature wildlife artist who is admired for her attention to sculpturing minute anatomically correct and functional details in her works. She will demonstrate carving a cougar head out of a double bar of soap.

Readings

Gingerich, J.L. *Florida's Fabulous Mammals.* World Publications. Tampa, FL. 1994.

Kobalenko, J. *Forest Cats of North America: Cougars, Bobcats and Lynx.* Firefly Books, Ltd. Willowdale, Ontario, Canada. Photos by T. Kitchin and V. Hurst. 1997.

Carving the Cougar

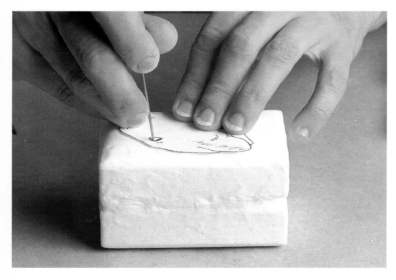

Glue two Ivory Soap bars together as described in Chapter One. Place side view pattern on the bar and trace outline. Locate the general positions of the eyes, ears, and mouth by punching tiny holes through the pattern on to the soap. Roughly shape that side to the drawn outline. Repeat on the other side.

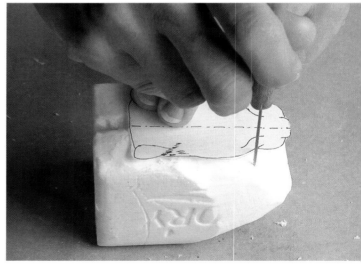

Outline the top view, keeping the pattern flat, and use a dissecting needle to transfer the outline.

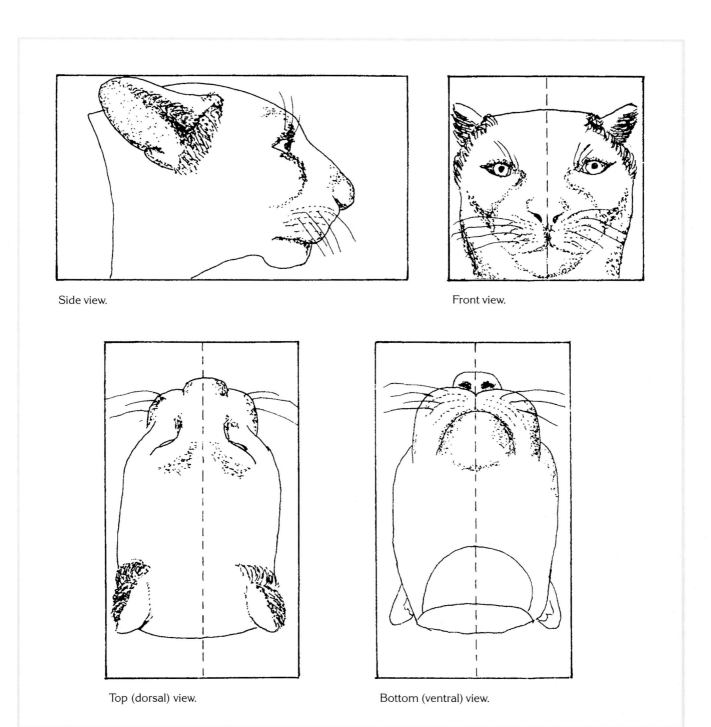

Side view.

Front view.

Top (dorsal) view.

Bottom (ventral) view.

Locate the ears on the top view by punching holes through the top pattern on to the soap.

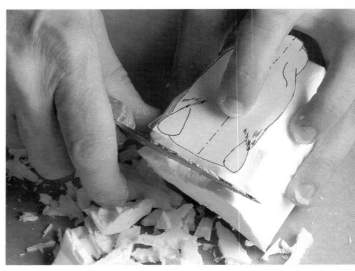

Remove the excess soap on the back of the head.

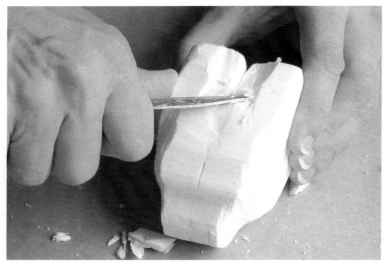

Shape the back of the head, being sure to preserve the ear lobes (pinnae).

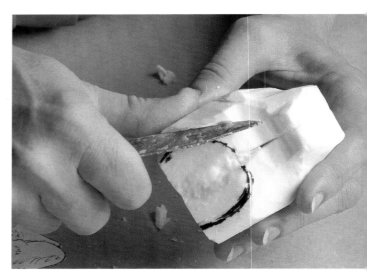

Outline the neck, and shape to blend with the cheek.

Make stop cuts along previously marked holes outlining the ear margins, and remove soap to stop cuts.

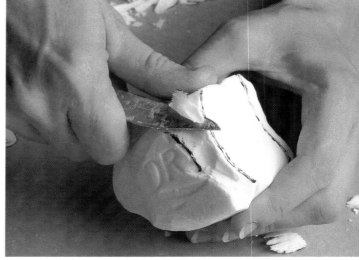

Mark the location of rear of jaw and rear view of neck, and blend together.

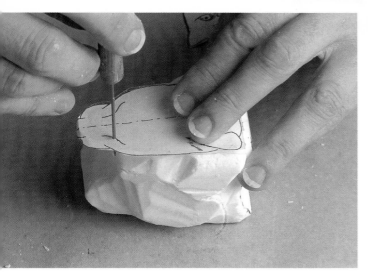

Locate the positions of the eyebrows from top view.

Transfer the location of the eyes from the side pattern showing medial (inner) and lateral (outer) margins, using the dissecting needle

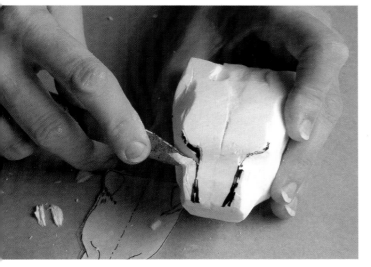

Mark the eyebrows and margins of the upper jaw/snout, and shape.

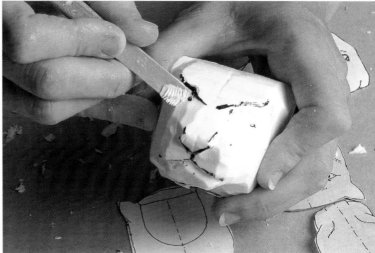

Make a concave cut on the right eye to mark the position of the inner corner of the eye. The margins of the left eye are shown as black dots. Carve the margins of the left eye also.

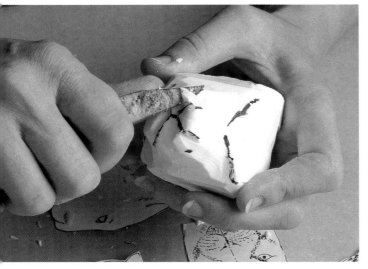

Mark positions of the nose and mouth. Start defining them.

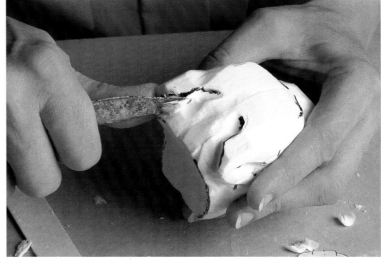

Block and shape the ears from both the side and top views, after again checking the margins of the ear lobes (pinnae).

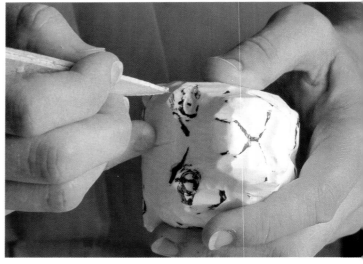

Find the center of the eye and carve the initial shape, the roundish eyeballs.

Mark hair tufts along front and outer margins of the pinnae. Then define inner edges of the ear margins blending with the location of the hair tufts (seen as black lines near the deep gouge).

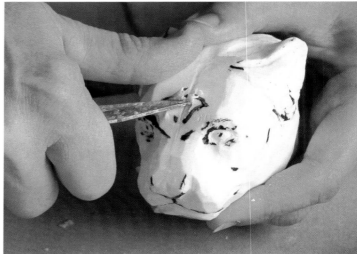

Mark and carve the eyebrow region.

Carving at this stage.

Mark and shape the cheeks.

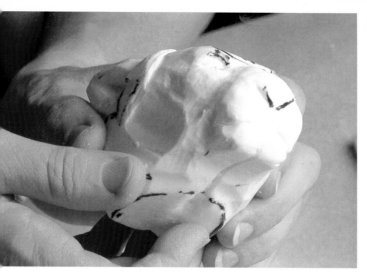

Appearance of the cheek, muzzle, and eyes at this stage.

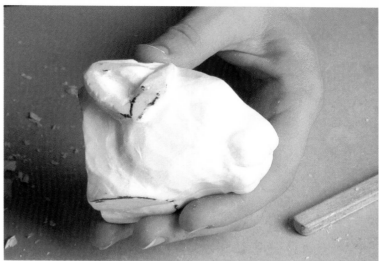

Side view of carving showing the blocked hair tuft area in front of the ears.

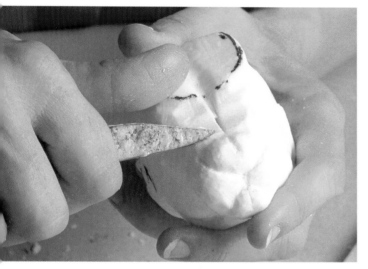

Carve the chin to a round shape, showing the indentation of skin at the hind margin of the chin.

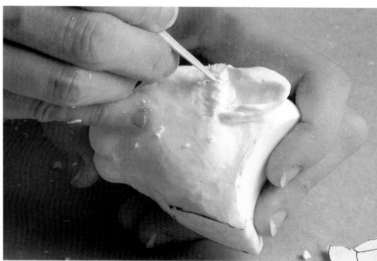

Shape inner surfaces of the pinnae and hair tufts on and in front of the ears.

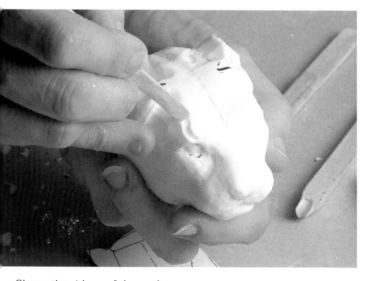

Shape the ridges of the eyebrows.

Make hair tufts by lightly scraping with a narrow, rounded tool.

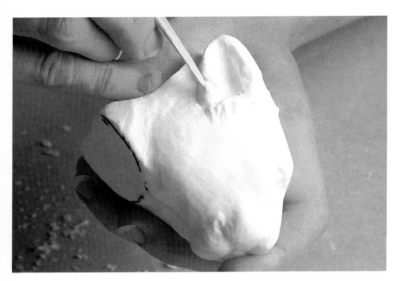

Note the shape of the small, fleshy lower lobe separated from the upper main ear lobe.

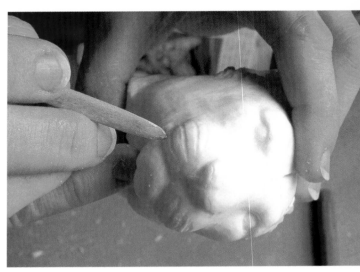

Make shallow fine grooves along sides of upper jaw for whisker tracts using a narrow rounded flat gouge. Whiskers will be located in the grooves.

Carve openings of the nostrils using a dissecting needle.

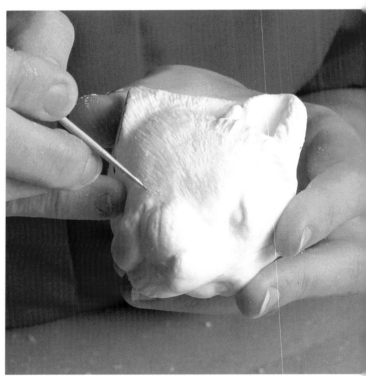

Make hair tracts by lightly etching the surface of the head using the sharp outer edges of a narrow rounded scraper. If you have a cat, examine it to help you determine the direction of the hair tracts.

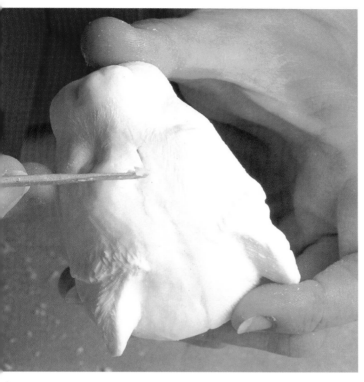

Fill in the joint line using the melded soap you previously made.

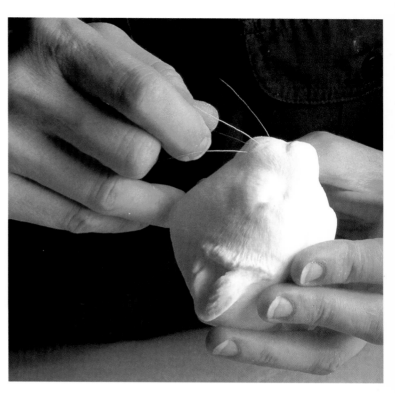

Make tiny holes in the grooves along the sides of the upper jaw. Pick up the previously selected measured hair and dip the base of the hair in a drop of craft glue (white or yellow wood glue is also suitable). Insert the hair with the glue into the hole. Bristles should be attached curving down and back. Attach about seven or eight hairs on each side.

Select white hairs and cut to about 1 1/2" in length from the tapered tips. Moose mane was used in this carving. It was purchased from a fly fishing shop that sold fly-tying materials. Other hairs may be substituted. Hairs best suited for simulating vibrissae should be stiff, slightly curved, and not hollow. Hairs shed by some dogs may be suitable. Bristles from some paint brushes may be used, but they often lack tapered tips.

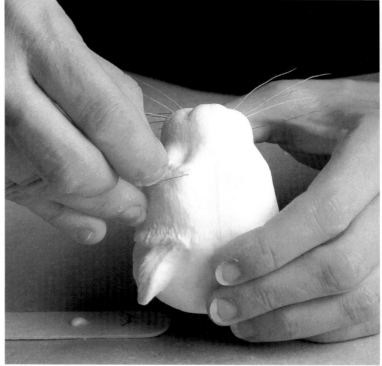

Attach about three or four shorter hairs (3/8 to 1/2 of an inch long) on the medial surfaces of the eyebrows.

Front view of finished mounted Cougar.

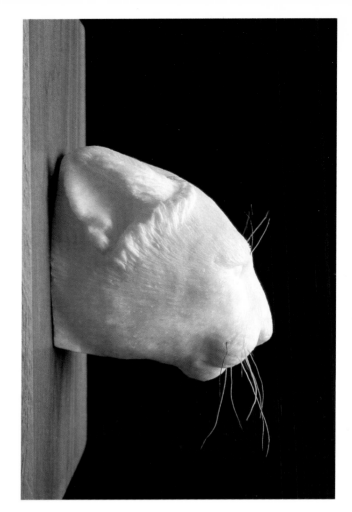

Side view of mounted Cougar

Oblique view of the mounted Cougar.

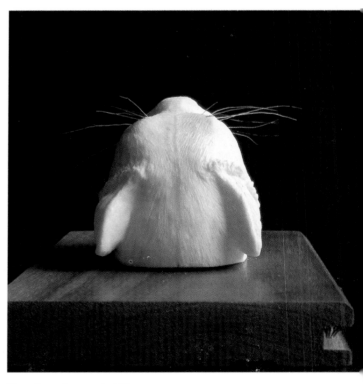

Top view of mounted Cougar.

Chapter 8: Orca, or Killer Whale

The Orca is a type of dolphin and is not a whale. They have worldwide distribution. They are particulary concentrated in large numbers in the British Columbia area of Canada. I recall seeing them as a child growing up in Southeastern Alaska as they moved in the channels adjacent to the island on which our town was located.

Only a pattern and completed soap carving is included here as the carver should be able to carve a breaching Orca from the information shown.

Additional Reading

Suzuki, Howard. *The Carver's Book of Aquatic Animals.* Schiffer Publishing, Ltd. Atglen, PA. 1995.

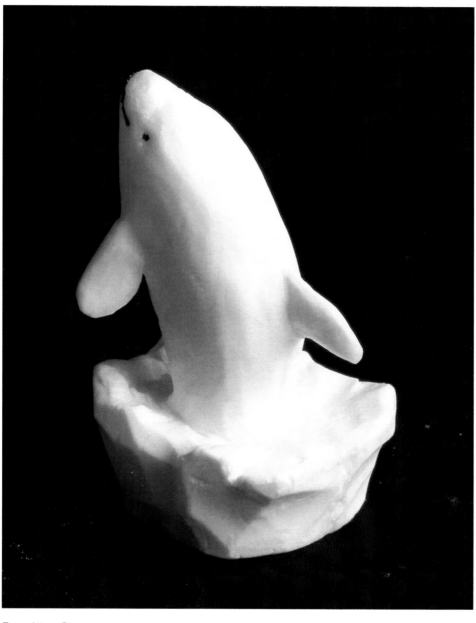

Breaching Orca.

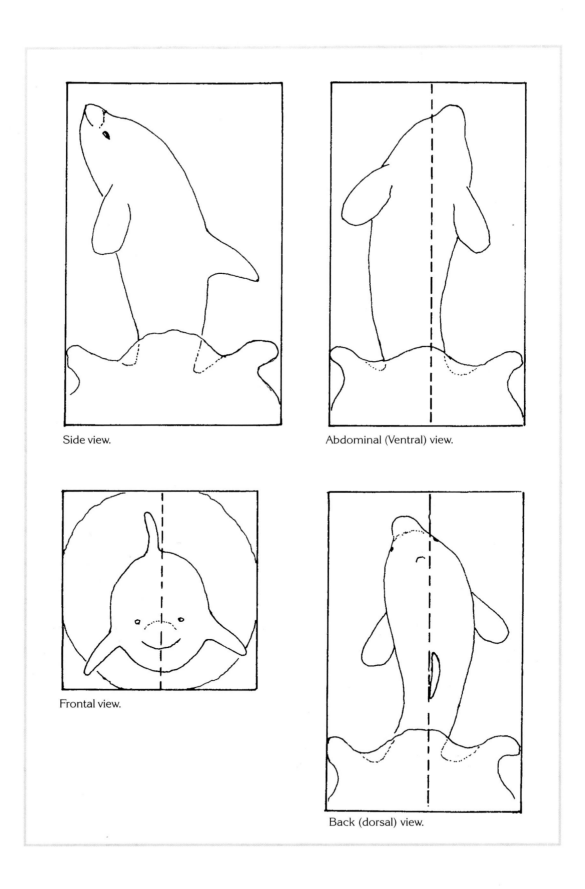

Side view.

Abdominal (Ventral) view.

Frontal view.

Back (dorsal) view.